Meet the Monsters
Activity Book

First published in Great Britain by HarperCollins Children's Books in 2009

13 5 7 9 10 8 6 4 2

ISBN: 978-0-00-784356-5

Monsters vs. Aliens TM & © 2009 DreamWorks Animation L.L.C.

Printed and bound in UK

DREAMWORKS

MONSTERS
VS
ALIENS

£1 with

happy meal

voucher

In restaurants
8th April – 12th May 2009
subject to availability.
Terms apply.

Meet the Monsters
Activity Book

Meet the Monsters
Activity Book

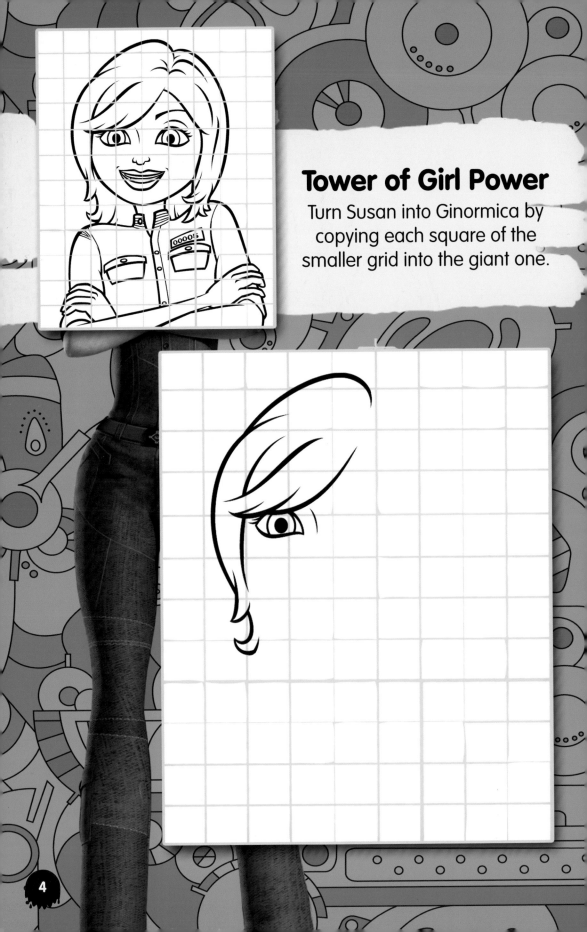

Tower of Girl Power

Turn Susan into Ginormica by copying each square of the smaller grid into the giant one.

4

Monsters to the rescue!

Incredible Inventions

Dr. Cockroach is a genius inventor!
If you could invent anything, what
would it be? Draw your
creation below.

Mirror Message

President Hathaway has ordered the Air Force to write a message to the robot in the sky, but they've done it the wrong way round! Can you work out what it says?

Answer:

_____

_____

_____

Find Your Inner Monster

You will need: Friends to play with, paper and pens

Create your own monsters with your friends. Each person draws a monster head at the top of their piece of paper, without showing anybody else.

Fold over the paper so just the neck is showing, then pass the paper to the person on your left.

Each person then draws the arms, body, legs and feet, folding the paper over and passing it on in the same way between each body part

Finally, unfold your pieces of paper to see what kind of monsters you have created!

The alien robot advances...

9

Earth, Full Speed Ahead

Gallaxhar is learning all about Earth before he begins his invasion. Help him by finding a word beginning with each letter in each category, in the grid below. The first one has been done for you.

	Name	Food	Animal	Place
E	Eric			
A				
R				
T				
H				

SUPER SECRET

B.O.B.
Gooey and Blue-y

Grossly Intellectual

Is your brain a match for Dr. Cockroach's?
Find out by completing this quiz.

1. B.O.B. stands for:
a) Bob. Obviously
b) Bicarbonate Ostylezene
   Benzoate
c) Big, oozing, blue

2. A cockroach is a(n):
a) Mammal
b) Reptile
c) Insect

3. San Francisco's most famous landmark is:
a) The Golden Gate Bridge
b) The Empire State Building
c) The White House

4. Who can shoot unbreakable silk from their nose?
a) Dr. Cockroach
b) B.O.B
c) Insectosaurus

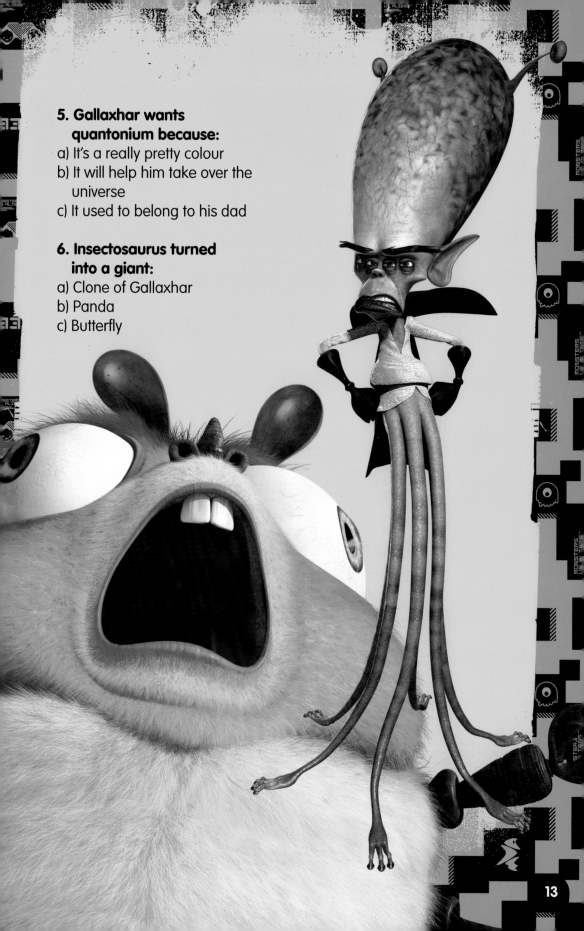

5. Gallaxhar wants quantonium because:

a) It's a really pretty colour

b) It will help him take over the universe

c) It used to belong to his dad

6. Insectosaurus turned into a giant:

a) Clone of Gallaxhar

b) Panda

c) Butterfly

Monstrous Crossword

Answer the clues below to complete this crossword puzzle.

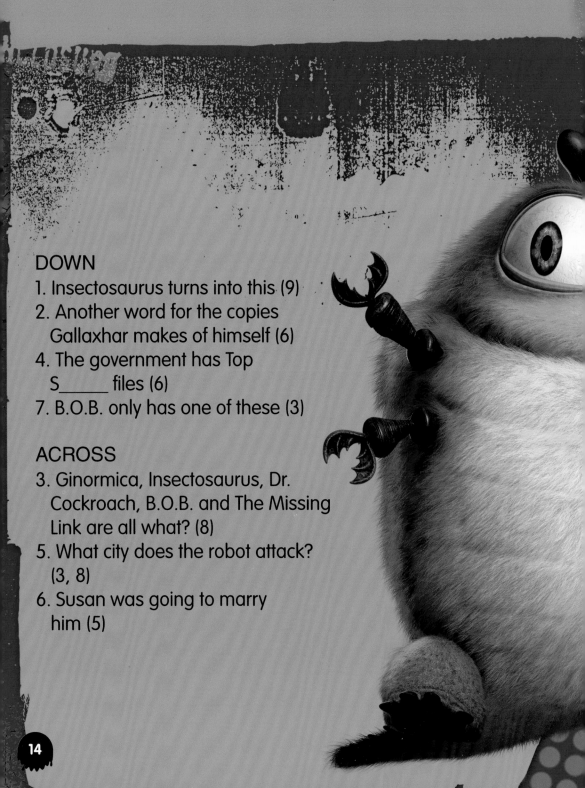

DOWN

1. Insectosaurus turns into this (9)
2. Another word for the copies Gallaxhar makes of himself (6)
4. The government has Top S_____ files (6)
7. B.O.B. only has one of these (3)

ACROSS

3. Ginormica, Insectosaurus, Dr. Cockroach, B.O.B. and The Missing Link are all what? (8)
5. What city does the robot attack? (3, 8)
6. Susan was going to marry him (5)

All in the Detail

Examine this picture of The Missing Link and Dr. Cockroach closely. Draw a line from the smaller details below to their place in the bigger picture.

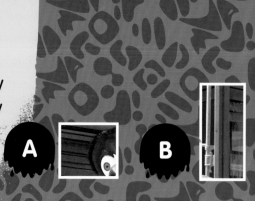

Dr. Cockroach:
Bug-Man

Monger's Report

General W. R. Monger needs to finish his report on the foiled alien invasion for the U.S Government files. There are some words missing. Choose words from the boxes below to complete the report.

Ginormica	Fish
Oozarama	Bones
School bus	Cocoon
Bunny rabbit	Skyscraper
Tentacles	Spaceship
Bridge	Banana
Robot	One hundred
Vermin	Gallaxhar
Butterfly	Bumblebee
Medal	Moonleader
Quantonium	Heads
Four	

We released the monsters called The Missing Link, B.O.B., Dr. Cockroach, Insectosaurus and _____ from prison to fight the alien _____. Although they managed to defeat the attacker, the Golden Gate _____ was badly damaged.

The evil alien named _____ has _____ eyes and eight _____. He captured Ginormica to remove the _____ from her body. However, the alien was unsuccessful and was crushed by a falling statue.

Finally, Insectosaurus turned into a giant _____. The monsters were rescued from the exploding alien _____.

I humbly suggest that the monsters receive a _____ in recognition of their service.

Sincerely,
W. R. Monger

Who is it?

Look closely at the pictures below. Who is below Ginormica, above The Missing Link and between Insectosaurus and Dr. Cockroach?

Write your answer here_____

The Missing Link:
Incredible Evolution!

Battle of the Biggest

Can you find eight differences between these two pictures of Insectosaurus and the alien robot?

Cockroach Clones

Dr. Cockroach got caught in Gallaxhar's cloning
machine! How many of him can you count here?

_____
Answer

Insectosaurus:
He's One Fluffy Bug

Gallaxhar's New Ship

Gallaxhar's spaceship was destroyed
when the monsters stopped him from
invading Earth. Design a new
one for him here.

Odd Ginormica Out

One of these pictures of Ginormica is slightly different to the others. Can you spot the odd Ginormica out?

Maze Mission

Help General W. R. Monger and Insectosaurus through the maze to rescue the other monsters.

START

END

Monster Memorise

Study the red items below for one minute, then cover them up. Draw as many as you can remember in the blue circle below.

The Missing Link's Moves

The Missing Link is practising his scary monster poses. Match the one below to the correct shadow.

Answers

Page 7
Mirror Message
Aliens, go home!

Page 12-13
Grossly Intellectual
1.b, 2.c, 3.a, 4.c, 5.b, 6.c.

Page 14-15
Monstrous Crossword

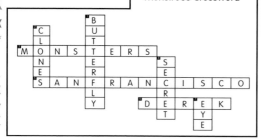

Page 16
All in the Detail

Page 18-19
Monger's Report

We released the monsters called The Missing Link, B.O.B., Dr. Cockroach, Insectosaurus and **Ginormica** from prison to fight the alien **robot**. Although they managed to defeat the attacker, the Golden Gate **Bridge** was badly damaged.

The evil alien named **Gallaxhar** has **four** eyes and eight **tentacles**. He captured Ginormica to remove the **quantonium** from her body. However, the alien was unsuccessful and was crushed by a falling statue.

Finally, Insectosaurus turned into a giant **butterfly**. The monsters were rescued from the exploding alien **spaceship**.

I humbly suggest that the monsters receive a **medal** in recognition of their service.

Sincerely,
W. R. Monger

Page 20
Who is it? Gallaxhar.

Page 22-23
Battle of the Biggest

Page 24
Cockroach Clones
There are 17
Dr. Cockroachs.

Page 27
Odd Ginormica Out
B is the odd one out.

Page 28
Maze Mission

Page 30
The Missing Link's Moves
D is the matching shadow.